3.95

"Now therefore ye are . . . built upon

the foundation of the apostles and prophets,

Jesus Christ himself being

the chief corner stone;

in whom all the building fitly framed

together groweth unto an holy temple in the Lord."

Ephesians 2:19–21

"That they may adorn the doctrine
of God our Saviour in
all things."
Titus 2:10

The Cornerstone Series

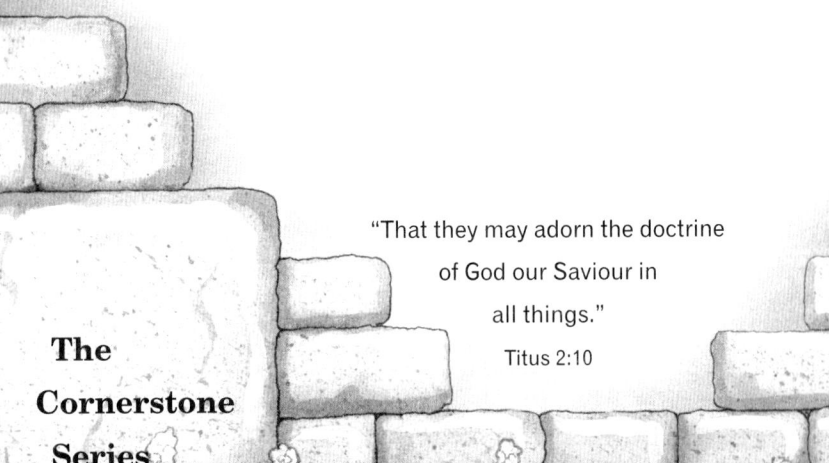

DYING to LIVE WITH CHRIST

By Merle Ruth

Rod and Staff Publishers, Inc.
P.O. Box 3, Hwy. 172
Crockett, Kentucky 41413
Telephone: (606) 522-4348

Copyright 1989

By Rod and Staff Publishers, Inc.
Crockett, Kentucky 41413

Printed in U.S.A.

ISBN 0-7399-0196-6
Catalog no. 2226

10 11 12 13 14 — 19 18 17 16 15 14 13 12 11 10

CONTENTS

Introduction
1. Dead to Self 9
2. Dead to Sin 29
3. Dead to the World 47
4. Risen With Christ 65

INTRODUCTION

"Whenever a command from God or other rightful authority arouses an inner rebellion, then is the time to make certain that you do not rebel, but obey. Unless you do, you are giving the tyrant self a longer lease at the very point where his hold is the strongest."

This paragraph, taken from the text of this book, speaks to man's most basic problem—self. As long as self is alive and in control of man's affections and will, doing right consistently and living the Christian life faithfully are not possible.

When men take the liberty to serve their own reason and will, they soon discover that there is trouble ahead. This develops frustrations and in turn, mental and emotional disorders.

Also, out of man's sinful nature, which all inherit at birth from Adam and their fathers, proceed hatred, variance, selfishness, greed, foolishness, unthankfulness, and much moral corruption.

Because men do not understand themselves and the underlying cause of their problems, they grasp for solutions as a drowning man grasps for straws in the water. All, however, ends in hopelessness, and therefore many decide that suicide is the answer. What a fearful plunge into the unknown darkness of eternity.

But, Friend, there is an answer. The author of this

book leads us to that answer in God's Word. Let God's Holy Spirit guide your mind into the realities of eternity as you study God's answer to man's most basic need. Until man finds this answer, all other solutions in his life are superficial.

Whether you are a church member or have had no use for God until now, the message of this book holds a blessing for you in bringing you to grips with your true self and the God who made and understands you perfectly. As you study, ask God to open your understanding of His Word and its message of most importance to you. He will. God bless you as you study.
—*The Publishers*

I am crucified with Christ: nevertheless I live; yet not I, but Christ liveth in me: and the life which I now live in the flesh I live by the faith of the Son of God, who loved me, and gave himself for me.
Galatians 2:20

1.

DEAD TO SELF

The women who arrived at the tomb of our Lord after He had risen were confronted with this question, "Why seek ye the living among the dead?" It may seem to the reader as though this treatise attempts to do that. Indeed, it does. For while it speaks often of dead people, those dead people are very much alive.

For a brief orientation, let us take a view of Calvary. On those three crosses were three men, all of whom experienced a different kind of death. The One on the central cross died *for* sin. One of the other two died *in* sin. The other died *to* sin.

Dying to Live With Christ

That third man—the repentant thief—typifies the category to which you and I ought to belong. The emphasis that this writing is placing on this kind of dying ought to make us newly aware of the paradoxical nature of the Christian life.

When something is paradoxical, it is characterized by apparent contradictions. This is so true of the Christian and the life that he lives. In fact, the very heart of Christianity—the crucifixion of our Lord—will stand forever as the supremely paradoxical event. It was, at the same time, the greatest of tragedies and the greatest of triumphs.

Now in relation to salvation, paradoxes exist not only in the realm of that which is provided, but also in the realm of experience. Take, for example, those words of Jesus: "Whosoever will save his life shall lose it: but whosoever will lose his life for my sake, the same shall save it" (Luke 9:24). That speaks of the paradoxical nature of the way into the Christian life.

When one is truly born again, he is born crucified. What a combination of terms! How seemingly contradictory. But not only is the Christian born crucified, the subsequent life that he lives is a crucified life. This fact is reflected in that memorable testimony

DEAD TO SELF

of Paul, the apostle: "I am crucified with Christ: nevertheless I live."

In God's new creation, life begins with death, and the ongoing life that follows is a crucified life. To the nonspiritual person, such terminology sounds like nonsense, but for those whose eyes have been opened, it is a concept that carries profound meaning. Although it is a difficult and highly spiritual concept, its practical implications get right to the heart of most, if not all, of our problems. Many of the problems that arise in our homes and in our churches can be traced to, or arise because of, a failure to live the crucified life.

So then, this expression "the crucified life" serves as one of the labels by which the genuine Christian life can be identified. It puts together in the same package a negative term and a positive term. But it mentions first, and thus gives priority to, the crucifixion aspect. There is a death that must precede the new life. On some trees the old leaves persist in hanging on until new buds push them off. Likewise, in the Christian experience we will die to self, sin, and the world only as we reckon ourselves dead to sin and alive unto God. In actual life, these two aspects of Christian experience cannot be separated, but in discussion we sometimes separate them for the

Dying to Live With Christ

purpose of emphasizing one or the other.

This writing, without apology, dwells at length on the dying aspect. This is an urgently needed emphasis. Human nature wants a religion that is made easy. Few are willing to pay the price of being good, but everyone wants to feel good.

The Christ whom many preach is a popular Christ, but their Christ is not a whole Christ. In Anabaptist thinking there was a sweet Christ and a bitter Christ, and they emphasized that the two must remain together. If we are to have Him as our Saviour, we must accept Him also as our Lord.

Christianity has in it two crosses—the Saviour's cross and the believer's cross. The former without the latter will avail nothing. Some groups make much of what God did for man, but not enough of what God wants to do in man.

Christianity truly interpreted has never been popular because it is so hard on self. There must of necessity be a dying to self, because in our natural state self is so very much alive. This entity called *self* has other names by which it is sometimes identified, such as *the carnal nature* or *the old man*. It is that center around which the whole of life once revolved.

DEAD TO SELF

Self is the idol we unknowingly worship in our preconversion days, but self is also man's greatest enemy and his nearest enemy. Martin Luther said, "I am more afraid of my own heart, than of the Pope and all his cardinals." Paul, the apostle, said, "I know that in me (that is, in my flesh,) dwelleth no good thing." Those are healthy attitudes; they are facts to which millions are blind.

In his natural state, man willingly worships self and has no desire whatever to depose self. He is blind to its real nature and fails to perceive the many ways in which self militates against his highest welfare.

How then does one arrive at the point where it can truly be said that he is dead to self? It begins when in one way or another the call of Christ reaches one's inmost being. "Come unto me . . . and I will give you rest" (Matthew 11:28). "Come ye after me, and I will make you to become fishers of men" (Mark 1:17). Hearing those calls, and others like them, will normally bring about an inward spiritual crisis.

This would possibly be an appropriate point at which to raise the question, How much inward struggle should be associated with genuine conversion? For obvious reasons this will not be the same in everyone's

Dying to Live With Christ

experience. But even when the conditioning has been excellent, there must come a period of crisis, and there must come a point of decision. This is because the call of Christ compels one to choose between self and Christ. And self and Christ are so unalike that saying yes to one demands saying no to the other.

So the person who is being pressed with the claims of Christ may hear from deep within a whole chorus of voices crying out in protest, "No, we will not have this man to reign over us." Out of that inner conflict may come a long, agonizing struggle. Knowing that he is not what he ought to be, the person may try a variety of ways to improve the quality of his life. Some people think that they can earn a ticket to heaven by being kind to their neighbors and by helping those in need. There are a lot of mistaken people who are trying by sheer will power and self-discipline to make themselves acceptable to God.

But the person who tries in these ways to make himself good enough for heaven is approaching God in the wrong way and is trying to do the impossible. God does not give inward peace to people who try to impress Him with their native goodness. Where that attitude exists, self can still be very much alive and even comfortable.

DEAD TO SELF

Romans 7 depicts this kind of struggle, and in that chapter the personal pronoun *I* appears repeatedly, showing that self is still on the throne. Any approach to God along these lines will culminate in either fatal despair or a cry of desperation, such as came from the heart of Saul of Tarsus: "O wretched man that I am! who shall deliver me from the body of this death [this deadly lower nature]?" That is really what he meant. Immediately after that cry of desperation, Paul throws the light of his victorious Christian experience upon that seemingly hopeless dilemma. "I thank God through Jesus Christ our Lord" (Romans 7:25).

Through Christ, Paul had found deliverance. Self can never cast out self, not even in the life of the regenerate one. But if we welcome the Christ of God into the temple where self has been enshrined, then the idol Self will fall as Dagon fell before the ark.

Many a person, before he submits to the crucifixion of the self-life, tries vainly to improve or change it—maybe even tries to convert it. There have been those who have thought that to get themselves out of the way, it was necessary to withdraw from society. So they denied themselves all natural human relationships and went out into the desert or into the mountain or into the

Dying to Live With Christ

hermit cell to fast, to labor, and to struggle in an effort to mortify the flesh.

While there is much to be said in favor of personal discipline, this approach is not the Bible-taught way to die to self. Self is altogether too tough to be killed in that way. Trying to Christianize self is a waste of time. Jesus said, "That which is born of the flesh is flesh" (John 3:6). It will remain flesh, regardless of how one may attempt to refine it or in any way improve it. Self is hopelessly evil. "The carnal mind," Paul says, "is enmity against God: for it is not subject to the law of God, neither indeed can be" (Romans 8:7). Since self cannot be converted, it must be crucified. In no other way can one experience deliverance from the tyranny of self.

Any manifestation of a self-righteous spirit or a self-justifying spirit betrays the fact that self is still being allowed to assert itself. Concerning the Jews of his day, Paul said: "They being ignorant of God's righteousness, and going about to establish their own righteousness, have not submitted themselves unto the righteousness of God" (Romans 10:3). But really, the Jews are not at all unique in that respect, are they? That is the universal human trait. In every person there is a deeply ingrained sense of self-sufficiency and self-righteousness. Jacob

DEAD TO SELF

was so self-confident that God finally had to cripple him in order to get him to lean on Him instead of on his own self-fed ingenuity. Not until then could God move in and fill the place in Jacob's life that self had so long occupied.

A young minister once addressed an aged backwoods Christian, whom he regarded as his inferior, with this question: "What do you think is the hardest thing in the Christian life?" Without even waiting for a reply, he continued by saying, "For myself, I think it is the requirement of denying one's sinful self."

"No," replied the wise old man, "the hardest thing is giving up one's righteous self," meaning, of course, his supposedly righteous self.

Of the two, I believe the old man's reply reflects the deepest insight into human nature and also into the nature of Christianity. That good opinion we have of ourselves is so hard to give up. We are probably more like King Saul than we realize. Instead of utterly destroying the Amalakites as he was told to do, he spared the best. However much we may want to spare the best of our self-life, God demands that it be all destroyed. The big *I* is anti-God and can never be harnessed to the purposes of God.

This route by which God calls us into the Christian

Dying to Live With Christ

life, this being brought under the control of Christ, has been called "the death route" because it so effectively puts to death the self within us. We deceive ourselves if we think we can afford to by-pass this death route. It cannot be done. In God's new economy, life comes out of death. That detour that so many take around this death route has been very properly called "life's most costly detour," and indeed it is. Before one can taste the abundant life, he must have a Calvary experience of his own.

One thing that contributes to the confusion that plagues today's religious world is the existence of so many watered-down perversions of Christianity. These watered-down perversions of Christianity, almost without exception, make room for the self-life.

The shocking extent to which self-idolatry is parading under the banner of Christianity is revealed in this statement made by one of today's most influential religious personalities: "A person is in hell when he has lost his self-esteem." That man's supposed gospel is aimed at inflating people's self-esteem. What a perversion of Christianity!

The late A. W. Tozer, in an article entitled "The Old Cross and the New," made the following observation.

DEAD TO SELF

"Unannounced and mostly undetected, there has come in modern times a new cross into popular evangelical circles. The new cross . . . lets Adam live without interference, his life motivation is unchanged. He still lives for his own pleasure; only now he takes delight in singing choruses and watching religious movies instead of singing worldly songs and drinking hard liquor. The new cross does not slay the sinner. It redirects him. It gears him into a cleaner and jollier way of living and saves his self-respect. To the self-assertive, it says, 'Come and assert yourself for Christ.' To the egoist, it says, 'Come and do your boasting in the Lord.' To the thrill-seeker, it says, 'Come and enjoy the thrill of Christian fellowship.' The Christian message is slanted in the direction of the current vogue in order to make it acceptable to the public."

The philosophy behind this thing may appear to be sincere, but its sincerity is deceptive. God offers life at the cross, but not an improved old life. The life He offers is life out of death. It always stands beyond the crucifixion experience at the cross.

How can this theology be translated into life? What does it demand from an awakened sinner? Simply this: he must repent and believe. He must forsake his sins

Dying to Live With Christ

and then go on to forsake himself. And the sinner can count on God to enable the doing of that which He requires.

The Gospel is the good news that God has already, in a provisional way, dealt our old self-life a fatal blow. Romans 6 makes this declaration: "Knowing this, that our old man is crucified with him, that the body of sin might be destroyed." There at Calvary God laid the groundwork for the devitalizing of self. The Colossians are told in chapter 3, verse 3: "For ye are dead, and your life is hid with Christ in God." This speaks of the divine ideal. That is how it is in the reckoning of God. Although I cannot explain it, I am convinced from these and other similar Scriptures that something was done in the work of Christ for us that now makes possible what otherwise would not have been possible. That self that otherwise could not be put to death can now be put to death. With God working in us and with the dynamics provided by God, we can now make actual what God in a provisional way has made possible. From the vantage point of our position in Christ and with the help and power of the Holy Spirit, we are to wage war against this enemy, self. It is not something we can do ourselves, but neither will God do it alone without our active cooperation. Without

DEAD TO SELF

God, we cannot. Without us, He will not. That is God's working principle in all His relating to man.

Two of the sayings of Jesus recorded by Luke are very pertinent to the point now in view. "And he said to them all, If any man will come after me, let him deny himself, and take up his cross daily, and follow me" (Luke 9:23). "If any man come to me, and hate not his father, and mother, and wife, and children, and brethren, and sisters, yea, and his own life also, he cannot be my disciple" (Luke 14:26). Clearly, the need to die to self is an integral part of answering Christ's call to discipleship. In the passage quoted from Luke 9, Jesus represents this as the first condition, and the latter passage indicates that it is to be the most costly of all conditions.

This call of Christ for self-denial often gets watered down. Contrary to popular opinions, it means much more than denying oneself this or that. Self is willing to be deprived of much, provided it is simply allowed to remain alive. The call of Jesus is a call to painful and lifelong self-renunciation. That naturally pitied, petted, pampered self must be dealt with harshly. It has rightly been said that when Christ calls a man, He bids him come and die. Only the man who is dead to his own will can truly follow Christ.

Dying to Live With Christ

You have possibly heard the saying, "In Christian experience, victory comes not by trying, but by dying." Rightly interpreted, that is a good statement, but it should not be used to encourage an irresponsible attitude. Putting self to death is a part of an active response to the call to discipleship. The passages from Luke quoted above give us not something to believe but something to do. They are addressed to the will.

Saving faith is a faith that works, that moves one to identify with Christ in such realistic terms that his former selfish pattern of life is radically interfered with. His life can never be the same. He is under new management. He lives no more to please himself, but rather to please Him who hath chosen him to be a soldier, and this will reflect itself in every detail of his life.

Dying to self is largely a matter of surrendering one's will to God's will. The prodigal son put self on the cross when he came to himself and said, "I will arise and go to my father" (Luke 15:18). When we give our initial yes to Christ, we must say no to self. That act must then be lengthened out into an attitude that says in every situation, "Not my will, but thine, be done" (Luke 22:42).

So then, dying to self is not a once-and-done matter. At conversion one must die to as much of self as he is

DEAD TO SELF

aware of at that point. But as we learn to know ourselves better, we will make new discoveries of the lingering presence of a reluctant-to-die self-life, and each new discovery calls for a new application of the disciplines of discipleship. It is significant that we are called upon to take up our cross daily. Paul's response to that was, "I die daily" (1 Corinthians 15:31). Included in the meaning of that would have been the fact that he was ready to have the Lord change his plans completely for the day. He refused to regard or respond to the insistence of self that it have its way.

From some source has come the idea that in every heart there is a throne and a cross. Ideally, at conversion self is removed from the throne and placed upon the cross. That removal requires the individual's working together with God. Then, in order to keep self on the cross, one needs to practice the various disciplines of discipleship. We can count on God to supply us with many opportunities to drive another nail to keep self crucified.

This truth is reflected in the following lines: "God may need to test you soon, / Just to keep your heart in tune." God may allow others to ignore our contribution. He may allow others to set at naught our good counsel. If we are sufficiently spiritual, we will see in such

Dying to Live With Christ

experiences new opportunities to affirm our deadness to the vain appeals of self. In some instances a very dislikable experience may be God's way of helping us to subdue the self-life.

Take, for example, plain, old-fashioned obedience. Being told what to do is very distasteful to self. Blessed is that person who can view his every act of obedience as an opportunity to strike another blow at this usurper, self.

Here are a few lines that hopefully will be helpful to the reader:

"Whenever a command from God or other rightful authority arouses an inner rebellion, then is the time to make certain that you do not rebel, but obey. Unless you do, you are giving the tyrant self a longer lease at the very point where his hold is the strongest."

The Bible urges wives to submit to their husbands. Happy is the wife who can perceive that obeying her husband when it is especially hard can be a means of conquering self for the Lord.

It is written of Christ, "He humbled [emptied] himself, and became obedient unto death" (Philippians 2:8). One empties himself when he does the thing that self does not want to do. The reason many people do not have victory is because they draw back from this death

DEAD TO SELF

route. They lack the moral courage and the spiritual fortitude required to wage a successful war against self. They do not have the heroic qualities that are needed to endure the pain and the suffering that it brings. The Bible says, "Forasmuch then as Christ hath suffered for us in the flesh, arm yourselves likewise with the same mind: for he that hath suffered in the flesh hath ceased from sin" (1 Peter 4:1). This suffering in the flesh is the experience of dying to self.

One saint made this observation: "There are many separated-from-the-world Christians who are not separated-from-themselves Christians." While we may recognize that that is one man's opinion, it is nevertheless a very disturbing thought, is it not? Might I still be clinging to self even after having let go of the world? Might that be possible? The sequence employed by our Lord in Luke 14:26 is very significant. One's "own life also" is named last, as though it will be the hardest thing to "hate."

Possibly few of us realize fully how an uncrucified self can stain and spoil one's service for the Lord.

It is reported of Michelangelo, a renowned artist, that when working at night, he wore over his head, fastened to his cap, a lighted candle in order that no

Dying to Live With Christ

shadow might fall on his work. To what lengths do we go to guard against the damaging effects of the shadow of self? Self dies hard. It is willing to make all kinds of concessions in order that it might be allowed to live. It will permit any number of rivals so long as it can be promised first place. It will consent to live anywhere if only its life is spared. But because it is so unreformable in character, it must not be spared.

Are there ways of determining whether I am dead to self? There are. Here is one test: Suppose you have been wronged; self will cry out for vengeance. As long as vengeance seems sweet, self is not dead. Again, as long as you swell in prosperity and shrink in adversity, that too is an indication that self is still active. But on the other hand, when you are forgotten, or neglected, or purposely set at naught, and you smile inwardly, glorying in the insult or oversight because you are thereby counted worthy to suffer with Christ—that is victory over self. When your good is evil spoken of, when your wishes are crossed, your tastes offended, your advice disregarded, your opinions ridiculed, and you take it all in patient loving silence—that too is victory over self. When you are content with any food, any raiment, any climate, any society, any solitude, any interruption by the will

DEAD TO SELF

of God, that also is victory over self.

Here is a personal testimony in the form of a poem.

NONE OF SELF AND ALL OF THEE

Oh, the bitter pain and sorrow
   That a time could ever be
When I proudly said to Jesus,
   "All of self and none of Thee."
Yet He found me; I beheld Him
   Bleeding on the accursed tree;
And my wistful heart said faintly,
   "Some of self and some of Thee."
Day by day His tender mercy—
   Healing, helping, full and free—
Brought me lower, while I whispered,
   "Less of self and more of Thee."
Higher than the highest heaven,
   Deeper than the deepest sea,
"Lord, Thy love at last has conquered—
   None of self and all of Thee."

How shall we, that are dead to sin, live any longer therein? . . . Knowing this, that our old man is crucified with him, that the body of sin might be destroyed, that henceforth we should not serve sin.
Romans 6:2, 6

For ye are dead, and your life is hid with Christ in God.
Colossians 3:3

2.

DEAD TO SIN

Another aspect of the crucified life is being dead to sin. Romans 6 has been called the *new birth chapter of Romans.* It is one way of looking at conversion and the life that follows. When comparing Romans 5 with Romans 6, one finds that Romans 5 is the justification chapter while Romans 6 is the sanctification chapter. God has not only justifying grace, but He also has sanctifying grace. He not only forgives the sinner, but He also changes him into a saint. In Romans 5 the accent is on Christ dying for the believer. In Romans 6 the accent is on the believer dying with Christ.

Dying to Live With Christ

Romans 5 shows that when an earnest seeker believes the Gospel, he is then justified freely by the boundless grace of God. This note comes through very clearly in the beginning of chapter 5. "Therefore being justified by faith, we have peace with God through our Lord Jesus Christ: by whom also we have access by faith into this grace wherein we stand, and rejoice in hope of the glory of God" (Romans 5:1, 2).

Paul anticipates that this emphasis on salvation by grace through faith, rather than by some legalistic keeping of some moral code, will be misinterpreted by some of his readers. They will reason thus: If where sin abounded, grace did much more abound, why not continue in sin?

Chapter 6 opens with Paul's response to this anticipated wrong conclusion. "What shall we say then? Shall we continue in sin, that grace may abound?" Some people would say, "Yes, continue in sin. The more we sin, the more the grace of God is called forth, and thus it is magnified and glorified."

Paul is moved of God to protest such reasoning. "God forbid. How shall we, that are dead to sin, live any longer therein? Know ye not, that so many of us as were baptized into Jesus Christ were baptized into his

DEAD TO SIN

death? Therefore we are buried with him by baptism into death: that like as Christ was raised up from the dead by the glory of the Father, even so we also should walk in newness of life. For if we have been planted together in the likeness of his death, we shall be also in the likeness of his resurrection: knowing this, that our old man is crucified with him, that the body of sin might be destroyed, that henceforth we should not serve sin. For he that is dead is freed from sin. Now if we be dead with Christ, we believe that we shall also live with him: knowing that Christ being raised from the dead dieth no more; death hath no more dominion over him. For in that he died, he died unto sin once: but in that he liveth, he liveth unto God. Likewise reckon ye also yourselves to be dead indeed unto sin, but alive unto God through Jesus Christ our Lord" (Romans 6:2–11).

This is God's answer to anyone who supposes that salvation by grace through faith allows for a permissive attitude toward sin. In effect, Paul says, "Away with the thought." Then he goes on to imply that such a conclusion reflects a measure of ignorance regarding God's plan of salvation. "Know ye not, that so many of us as were baptized into Jesus Christ were baptized into his death?" (Romans 6:3). Here he is saying, "If

Dying to Live With Christ

you think that being a Christian and continuing in sin are compatible, then you are reflecting an ignorance of something very basic in God's plan."

So then, victory over sin begins with knowing. It is important that we know the plan of salvation. It is true that our Christian experience grows out of our faith, but our faith grows out of our knowledge. If there is a provision God has made that we do not know about, we will not reckon on that, and consequently, we will be the loser.

After Abraham Lincoln had issued the Emancipation Proclamation, some slaves continued on in slavery. Some went into hiding because they did not know that lawfully they were free. They were ignorant of the knowledge that could have meant their freedom. Slavery to sin is likewise related to ignorance of the things of God.

The divinely inspired writer of Romans 6 was then led to emphasize in particular one truth that we need to know in order to stop sinning. One must know about the believer's divinely provided union with Christ. There is possibly no other portion of the Bible that focuses so sharply on this hard-to-explain yet gloriously real union—the union of the believer with the triumphant Christ. As one meets the conditions for salvation, he is

DEAD TO SIN

"baptized into Jesus Christ." This word *baptized* means "to be brought under control of." Those Israelites who were baptized unto Moses in the Red Sea came under his control, under his management. There was a transfer of ownership; they now belonged to him. Just so, as one is baptized into Jesus Christ, he likewise comes under His control. That is the divine ideal.

In the foregoing paragraph, which baptism is in focus—the ordinance of Water Baptism or Holy Spirit baptism? The answer should be obvious. Mere water baptism, which is symbol baptism, can never baptize one into Jesus Christ. The baptism spoken of here is the same as is referred to in 1 Corinthians 12:13: "For by one Spirit are we all baptized into one body." That body is the mystical body of Christ, the church. Although water baptism is an essential act of obedience, it cannot, however correct the mode may be, baptize one into Jesus Christ. That miracle of being joined to the living Christ occurs at conversion when, without human hands, one is baptized with the Holy Spirit.

Notice that verse 3 of Romans 6 speaks both of being "baptized into Jesus Christ" and being "baptized into his death." God has made possible such a vital union between the believer and Christ that the believer

Dying to Live With Christ

receives a new outlook and a new purpose in life. Because Christ died for his sin, the believer, as he becomes one with Christ, feels impelled to die to sin. He comes to realize that Jesus died as much to keep him from sinning as He died to pardon his sins. The angel said, "Thou shalt call his name Jesus: for he shall save his people from their sins" (Matthew 1:21). That means more than simply the removal of guilt. It means deliverance from the practice of sin. That deliverance is possible through union with Christ. On God's side, that union is effected by the repentant one being baptized with the Holy Spirit. God does this in response to the faith of the repentant. By that miracle, the believer is united to Christ in a spiritual way.

Growing out of that should come, on the experiential side, a personal relationship with the Lord Jesus Christ. If that personal relationship is anywise near the divine ideal, it will be so dynamic that the believing one feels inwardly impelled to stop the sinning business. Any faith that fails to do that is not saving faith.

The thrust of Romans 6 is that being saved necessitates being holy, for it results in such close identification with the living Saviour that one becomes dead to the things that Christ is dead to.

DEAD TO SIN

If you would ask me, "What is the supremely distinctive mark of the Christian religion? What is it that makes Christianity tower so far above other religions?" my answer would likely be, "God's act of joining every new believer to the Lord Jesus." Then as the new believer reckons on this divinely revealed reality, he develops a personal relationship with the Lord Jesus. He begins to appropriate the newly received power of the Holy Spirit. This is how one becomes dead to sin.

Notice the expression in verse 8: "Now if we be dead with Christ . . ." That is how we become dead to sin. Just as Christ died and rose again and is forever different, we are so to identify with Him that we die to the old life and become forever different. So the death and resurrection of Jesus serve as both the provision of salvation and the pattern of sanctification. Holiness becomes possible only as one becomes dead with Christ and then lives the crucified life.

Normally, the only way out of any world is by way of death. The only way out of the world of sin is by becoming dead with Christ, for it is thus that we become dead to all that He is dead to. Verse 7 speaks to this point: "For he that is dead is freed from sin." We become free from sin by becoming dead with Christ.

Dying to Live With Christ

So the crucified life is a life that is dead not only to self, as was emphasized in the first chapter, but also to sin. Both self and sin are enemies of holiness. Between them there is a very close relationship. However, they can be treated separately, at least on the discussion level.

The last verse of the passage in focus, Romans 6:11, lays upon us one of the disciplines that must be cultivated. "Likewise reckon ye also yourselves to be dead indeed unto sin." Dead men do not respond. One who is dead with Christ does not respond to the attraction and appeal of sin. He sees sin through the eyes of Christ, stripped of all that attractive veneer with which the devil covers it, and consequently he, like Christ, abhors sin. Men who are dead to sin respond to its enticements in the words of Joseph, "How . . . can I do this great wickedness, and sin against God?" It is repulsive to them.

Sin, like self, has a very wide spectrum. There are inward sins and outward sins. There are sins of commission; there are sins of omission. There are sins of the flesh, and there are sins of the spirit. One can sin in action, in attitude, and in appearance. God hates even the proud look.

The prodigal son sinned in one way; his elder brother sinned in another way. The elder brother's sins were

DEAD TO SIN

largely sins of disposition. We can sin by being contentious, jealous, defensive, and by simply manifesting a hard-to-please disposition. It is very probable that in God's sight, the elder brother was as great a sinner as the prodigal.

In some people's belief there is a category called respectable sins. They are the kind that never get you in trouble with the law. They are the kind that one can even take to church. They are the kind that can even stand behind the church pulpit. But in God's reckoning, there is no such thing as a respectable sin.

Sin often goes unrecognized. One reason for this lies in the fact that Satan does his best to hide sin behind a beautiful disguise. Satan can make some sins look as though they came straight from heaven.

Secondly, many sins are a perversion of something basically good. That is another reason why we sometimes fail to recognize sin as sin. It is not a sin to eat, but to overeat is a sin. According to Romans 6, the key to victory over all these forms of sin is our becoming dead with Christ.

I would like to emphasize now the significance of that little word *with*—"dead with Christ." That word signifies that salvation is essentially a personal relationship with the Lord Jesus Christ. It is a wrong concept to

Dying to Live With Christ

view salvation as a package that one receives and then walks away with. No, getting saved and living in victory over sin demands the establishment of a personal relationship with the Lord Jesus Christ. By faith we need to make actual in an experiential way that which God by grace made possible in a provisional way.

It is true that in the religious world there has always been a commodity known as *cheap grace*. *Cheap grace* allows one to drag his sins with him even as he supposedly identifies with Christ. But really, *cheap grace* is not grace at all. It is a devil-sanctioned substitute for God's grace. Salvation is free, but salvation is not cheap. On the Godward side, it was provided at enormous cost; and on the manward side, it is experienced only by those who are willing to pay the cost of discipleship. So let us distinguish between salvation being free and it being cheap. It was costly to God to provide it, and it is costly on the part of man to experience it.

Christian discipleship, as was just implied, is one of the labels for identifying the life that is lived in union with Christ. It is a personal, daily, practical identifying of one's self with the holiest of all persons whose oft-repeated requirement is: "Be ye holy; for I am holy." And "Can two walk together, except they be agreed?" So the

DEAD TO SIN

Christian walk is a holy walk with a holy Person. This is Christian discipleship, and it spells death to sin. The believer's establishing of this relationship brings about in him a dying to sin.

At one point especially, Peter's discipleship became defective. That was when he followed afar off. Whenever one begins to follow afar off, he begins to acquire a certain blindness toward sin. And the sins most likely to go unrecognized are his own. It is therefore imperative that we cultivate our divinely-made-possible oneness with Christ. Things take on a more accurate appearance as we get close to the Lord.

The prophet Isaiah, even though he lived in the Old Testament era, had an experience that serves to illustrate this truth. In chapter 5 of his writings, we hear him pronounce woe after woe upon his fellow countrymen, and rightly so. But after his vision of the thrice-holy God, described at the beginning of chapter 6, we hear him pronouncing a woe upon himself. "Woe is me! for I am undone; . . . I am a man of unclean lips." We need to become honest enough to call sin, sin, before we can die to it.

Standing near the beginning of Colossians 3 is another passage that elaborates on how being "dead with

Dying to Live With Christ

Christ" makes possible victory over sin. "For ye are dead, and your life is hid with Christ in God. When Christ, who is our life, shall appear, then shall ye also appear with him in glory. Mortify therefore your members which are upon the earth; fornication, uncleanness, inordinate affection, evil concupiscence, and covetousness, which is idolatry" (Colossians 3:3–5). God has provided that the body of sin, the sin potential in the believer, can be rendered inoperative. "Our old man is crucified with him" (Romans 6:6). We are therefore to bring our condition into conformity with our position in Christ. This command to mortify our sins is a call to cooperate with God in the carrying out of the death sentence against sin. The word *mortify* means "put to death." Every sinful thought that wants to spring into action, we are to put to death. Even the thought itself must not be entertained.

New believers at Ephesus burned the books they had once used. Sin needs to receive from us that same kind of treatment. It needs to be destroyed. All relationships with it must be severed. There must be in us no response to its appeal. Jesus died *for* our sins so that we might be able to die *to* them. We can experience more than simply forgiveness of sins committed. God wants us to experience release from sin's power!

DEAD TO SIN

By God's grace we can do whatever we ought to do. Mark that down. God never calls upon us to do what we cannot do. But it does require laying hold upon the grace that He makes available. We are not left to our own resources, to do this in our own strength. Philippians 2:13 contains this good news: God works in you to perform His pleasure. But although God does work in you, He does not work instead of you. Let us not blur that distinction. God will work in us to enable us to do our part, but there is a part He will not do. But He will give us the power to do it. He works "in you," but not instead of you.

Let us take a closer look now at this idea of reckoning ourselves dead indeed unto sin. Being dead to sin with Christ is a faith position. It is by means of our faith that we reckon ourselves to be dead to sin. Reckoning is not acting as if it were so; it is acting because it is so. "How firm a foundation, ye saints of the Lord, / Is laid for your faith in His excellent Word!" We have a firm foundation. We have something to reckon on. We ought to rejoice in the foundation that God our Saviour has given us to reckon on. So numerous and adequate are the provisions that Paul was moved to speak of our being "more than conquerors."

Now what, specifically, does saving faith reckon on?

Dying to Live With Christ

Putting it briefly, saving faith reckons on the finished work of Christ. It reckons on the pardoning, cleansing power of the blood. It reckons on the illuminating power of the Word. It reckons on the sanctifying presence of the Holy Spirit. It reckons on the renewing power of Christian fellowship. It reckons on all the multiplied means of grace. In short, it reckons on the glorious possibility that one can live in victory over sin.

In the time of the Caesars, a Roman armada sailed out of the Mediterranean Sea toward the British Isles. Their mission was to invade the British Isles. When the enemy vessels appeared, thousands upon thousands of Englishmen turned out to defend their country, but they were shocked by the sight that met their eyes. After disembarking their ships, the Romans deliberately set them on fire, thus cutting themselves off from any possible means of escape. What were they doing? They were reckoning on victory, and in that, we can learn from them.

Elsewhere in Romans we receive this command: "Put ye on the Lord Jesus Christ, and make not provision for the flesh, to fulfil the lusts thereof" (Romans 13:14). In modern terminology that means "burn your bridges behind you." Burn those bridges over which you might be tempted to turn back into the old life of sin. Avoid

DEAD TO SIN

the paths that lead to temptation. Guard the gates to your mind. Keep out of bad company. Stay away from questionable places. If you do not want the fruit of sin, stay out of the devil's marketplace. Or to change the figure, "We have too much dynamite in us to walk close to the flames of sin." All of this is involved with dying to sin.

Being dead to sin also necessitates imposing a strict discipline upon one's body. Originally, all bodily appetites and drives were good, very good. But through the Fall, human nature became so twisted that there is now a tendency toward excess and perversion. Although the seat of sin is deeper than the body, the body can and often does become the instrument of one's inborn sin.

One writer states it thus: "Sin originates in our Adamic nature and operates in our physical body." Romans 6:13 records this warning: "Neither yield ye your members as instruments of unrighteousness unto sin." So bodily discipline is involved in dying to sin.

Some of the sternest words ever spoken by Jesus call for this kind of discipline. "If thy right eye offend thee, pluck it out. . . . If thy right hand offend thee, cut it off." The evident meaning of Jesus is that to impose upon your body a stern discipline in this life is better than being lost forever in the torments of hell

Dying to Live With Christ

as a consequence of loose living. The best of saints are not exempt from the necessity to exercise this kind of control. "I keep under my body," Paul writes, "and bring it into subjection: lest . . . when I have preached to others, I myself should be a castaway" (1 Corinthians 9:27). If Paul needed to exercise this discipline; who among us dare plead for exemption?

Let us turn now to a passage that speaks of the dynamic that is available for the exercise of this discipline. Romans 8:13 says, "For if ye live after the flesh, ye shall die." The death in view here must be spiritual death because everyone, regardless of how he lives, dies physically. Then comes the glorious part of that verse: "But if ye through the Spirit do mortify the deeds of the body, ye shall live." We can have unending life. We can be made free from the reign of sin by the counteracting power of the Holy Spirit. But His presence must be allowed to penetrate our lives.

However, instead of seeking to have more of the Spirit, it is better to think in terms of yielding more of ourselves to the control of the Spirit. As we through the Scriptures become aware of areas of self not yet surrendered to Christ, we yield them to His control also. This is the secret to victorious living, for it is He

DEAD TO SIN

that brings into one's life the power and presence of the living, victorious Christ.

Paul's testimony can be ours: "The law of the Spirit of life in Christ Jesus hath made me free from the law of sin and death" (Romans 8:2). In this testimony, the term *law* means "principle." Paul is saying, "I have been delivered from the principle of sin by the principle of life that is now operating in me." You too can count on God to work with you to devitalize the sin principle in your life. That is the good news of the Gospel and a very indispensable part of it. It is not enough to know that the guilt we incurred can be removed. We need to lay hold of the truth that we can be delivered also from the power of sin.

So for the Christian, sinning is never a necessity. All casualties in the Christian experience are of the avoidable kind.

The key to victory over sin lies not alone in our deadness to sin, but also in our aliveness to God. This latter concept will get more attention at a later point. It is simply introduced here as a balancing truth. Unless one cultivates a love relationship with the living Christ, it will be well nigh impossible to give up the sin to which one is attached. If we do not have this positive dimension in our experience, it is going to be well nigh impossible to

Dying to Live With Christ

break the hold of sin. It is the expulsive power of the new affection that will break the affection we had for sin.

However, in the school of God one never graduates from the dead-with-Christ stage. We make progress spiritually only as the negative and the positive remain together. One must be at the same time dead with Christ and alive unto God. If we do not feed the new man, we will not have enough strength to overcome the old man. So the two need to go together.

And now, a clarifying note, and may it serve also as a warning. Although it is gloriously possible to be dead to sin, sin itself remains alive. Even though it has no rightful claim upon you and me, and even though it receives no response from us, it will continue to appeal for our attention. By the same token, we may be through with the devil, but the devil is not through with us. So our spiritual survival demands that we put on the whole armor of God, that we watch and pray, and that we do not knowingly tolerate any sin in our lives.

"Let not sin therefore reign in your mortal body" (Romans 6:12). We were redeemed from ruin in order that we might reign over the sin that once reigned over us. Romans 5:17 speaks of reigning "in life by one, Jesus Christ."

3.

DEAD TO THE WORLD

Ideally, the Christian is dead, not only to self and to sin, but also to the world.

But why be dead to the world? What is wrong with the world? Are we not all a part of the world? The early Anabaptists would have been quick to reply, "No!" They held to a two-kingdom theology that drew a sharp line between the church and the world.

In this respect, some present-day Mennonites have changed radically. A very influential Mennonite leader has made this assertion: "One of the recent changes in Mennonite thinking is the realization that we are both

Dying to Live With Christ

in the world and *of* the world." Yes, it is urgent that we reaffirm the need that we be dead to the world.

Some might raise other questions. How is this proposition to be reconciled with the fact that "God so loved the world, that he gave his only begotten Son" for it? Did not Jesus say, "As my Father hath sent me, even so send I you" (implying, into the world)? Is it possible, at the same time, to both reach the world and be dead to the world? Why the seemingly opposite nature of some New Testament commands? In one instance, "Come out from among them" (2 Corinthians 6:17); in another, "Go ye into all the world" (Mark 16:15).

For the Spirit-taught, Bible-taught Christian, that apparent contradiction is not difficult to resolve. One key to its solution is recognizing that in the New Testament the word *world* has different meanings. In every instance, the context in which the word appears helps one to select the right meaning.

The aspect of the world that God loves is the people aspect. God sees them as His sons and daughters, by creation. He sees how the devil has deceived them and how sadly they are suffering from the plague of sin. He is moved, by who they are and by who He is, to love them. As the nature of God is restored to us through

DEAD TO THE WORLD

regeneration, we too ought to be moved to sacrifice for the sake of God's many prodigal sons and daughters.

But there is likewise an aspect of the world that God cannot love. He is pained by man's unmindfulness of his Creator and Provider. The disregard shown for the great sacrifice made on Calvary's cross is doubtlessly appalling to God. The keen eye of God sees on every side the ugly evils of pride, selfishness, stubbornness, greed, hate, violence, lust, oppression, and suchlike.

This aspect of the world is morally incompatible with the holy nature of God. He will tolerate it only for a time. Man's yielding to sin and Satan has produced a culture, a system—a worldly way of life that stands at enmity with God. As such, it is also the enemy of holiness and a threat to God's children. This, then, is the world to which we must die.

When we talk of being "dead to the world," we are not endeavoring to say, by that one expression, all that can be said about the believer's relation to the world. That is just one aspect of it. But it is a vital one and a much neglected one.

If, however, we want to think in terms of the believer's total relation to the world, we need to bring into service these three terms: separation, illumination,

Dying to Live With Christ

and evangelization. Obviously, being dead to the world relates to the separation aspect of our relation to the world. Being dead to the world does not mean we are insensitive to its needs. We can be, and if we are, then we are dead to the world in the wrong way. In fact, the presence of an attitude of indifference would indicate that we have imbibed the spirit of the world, and have drifted back into the world ourselves. The only right way for the Christian to be dead to the world is for him to be dead to the evils of the world. Unless one is dead to the evils of the world, he cannot exert upon the world a redemptive influence.

Here is another sidelight. We do not have to live in geographical isolation in order to be dead to the world. Jesus was dead to the world in the right sense, yet constantly rubbed shoulders with it. But He also spent whole nights in communion with His heavenly Father.

For us, there is surely such a thing as an unbalanced exposure to the world. It is only as we spend time with God and with the people of God that we can safely rub shoulders with the world and at the same time be safeguarded against the evils of the world.

It has long been recognized and is widely acknowledged that the Christian's opposition arises from the world, the

DEAD TO THE WORLD

flesh, and the devil. We sometimes sing the question, "Is this vile world a friend to grace, / To help me on to God?" Judging from the way some professing Christians relate to the world, one might suppose it is. In order to deceive, the world can put on a very captivating smile. But in the Bible the true character of the world stands exposed.

In a letter to professing Christians, one of God's servants was moved to sound this note of warning: "Ye adulterers and adulteresses, know ye not that the friendship of the world is enmity with God? whosoever therefore will be a friend of the world is the enemy of God" (James 4:4). The only possible deduction one can make from that is that there must exist between the world's system and God an underlying antagonism, a moral incompatibility.

Did not Jesus on one occasion say, "That which is highly esteemed among men is abomination in the sight of God"? (Luke 16:15). He surely did. This antagonism that exists between the two kingdoms is accountable to the fact that Satan is the god of this world. But there is more behind it than that.

What did God tell Satan after our first parents had bowed to him? God said, "I will put enmity between thee and the woman, and between thy seed and her seed"

Dying to Live With Christ

(Genesis 3:15). God put that enmity there. This fact is often overlooked. It is by divine decree that this enmity exists between the two kingdoms. This God-declared war is His way of preventing moral confusion in a social order that embraces elements that are of an opposite nature.

Lest we become too friendly with the world, God also reminds us in Galatians 1:4 that Christ "gave himself for our sins, that he might deliver us from this present evil world." If the world is as harmless as some claim it to be, why would Deity have made so great a sacrifice to rescue men and women from the clutches of the world?

In John 17 there is a recorded prayer of our Lord. This heart cry of the Saviour reflects how He sought to build into His followers proper convictions regarding the world.

In verse 6, we read, "I have manifested thy name unto the men which thou gavest me out of the world." If we truly appreciate our deliverance from the world, it will be evidenced by our refusal to return into the world.

Verse 15 states, "I pray not that thou shouldest take them out of the world, but that thou shouldest keep them from the evil." Being in the world is like being in enemy territory, and therefore necessitates being divinely kept from the evil of the world.

DEAD TO THE WORLD

Verse 16 records, "They are not of the world, even as I am not of the world." God wants us to relate to the world as His Son did. That means being in the world geographically, but not spiritually. We are to view ourselves primarily as citizens of heaven. One of the biggest challenges we face is how to be in the world, but not of the world.

Consider this question: Where is the character of the world best seen? We have already stated that in the Bible the true character of the world stands exposed, but getting more specific, the answer would be "at Calvary, when the world crucified its would-be Saviour." There on Calvary the proud world spoke its mind out loud. The cross perfectly portrays the world's thoughts of Christ. How then can we be on good terms with the world that crucified our Saviour?

Some might claim that the world has changed, that the world has improved, that the world today would welcome the Saviour with open arms. Well, if you believe that, you know neither human nature nor the world. The world would crucify Christ as readily today, if He lived here in bodily form, as they did over nineteen hundred years ago. It probably would not use a wooden cross, but it would treat Him as badly as it could. In fact, it is presently doing that very thing.

Dying to Live With Christ

Remember the day when a voice from heaven said, "Saul, Saul, why persecutest thou me?" Every time he beat a Christian, Saul was beating Christ. In that sense, Christ is being beaten today and every day in widely scattered parts of the world.

No doubt we would be surprised if we knew the amount of scorn and ridicule that is heaped upon our Lord Jesus every day right here in America. However, our biggest surprise would most likely be if we knew how much our Saviour is denied and wounded by churchgoing people who are not dead to the world.

Yes, the character of the world is evil, and the appeal of the world is real. With its disarming appeal, the world has swallowed up many one-time believers.

Lot lost nearly everything to the world. Demas lost it all; he sacrificed his soul on the altar of the world.

The nearer one gets to the world, the stronger the pull of the world becomes. Its attractions are very glittering. It is patient, and yet it is persistent. It has many tactics. In order to captivate the unsuspecting, it stoops even to compromise. It has a philosophy which says, "If you can't beat them, join them." So it sends out many wolves in sheep's clothing. Like the Gibeonites, it has a very disarming approach. Instead of appealing to

DEAD TO THE WORLD

the baser appetites of the Israelites, they appealed to their good qualities. They appealed to their sympathy, their compassion; and consequently, they deceived the Israelite leaders.

The world will likewise direct its appeal to that which is highest and best among Christians. "Look at how wonderfully humanitarian we are. Here is a list of people we have helped. Our organization needs people like you. Imagine what a contribution you can make through our channels." Those who are spiritual recognize that we have less to fear from the frowns of the world than we do from the smiles of the world.

The pull of the world is resistible by God's grace. If you are a saint of God living up to your spiritual potential, those appeals of the world will fall upon deaf ears. The most useful saints are those least attracted by the world. God has given them the power to see through the disguise the world wears. Someone said this about one of God's servants: "There was nothing in the world that held the slightest attraction to him."

If we are truly dead to the world, we will experience what Paul, the apostle, spoke of in his testimony recorded in Galatians 6:14: "God forbid that I should glory, save in the cross of our Lord Jesus Christ, by

Dying to Live With Christ

whom the world is crucified unto me, and I unto the world." All the ties between Paul and the world had been severed. It was to him a dead thing, and he was to it a dead man. Paul had lost his esteem for the world. No longer did he value her opinions and judgments. He judged her as being no longer worth listening to.

Paul looked out upon the world which thought so highly of itself, and in effect said this: "I have lost all respect for you; you are so blind and wicked that you crucified your Best Friend. In nothing is your judgment reliable. You call me a babbler; so what—I could not care less about your opinion." That was Paul's attitude toward the world.

Can you, with respect to the world, make a claim like that? How unlike Paul many professing Christians are!

How do we become dead to the world? One Christian gave a new convert these instructions: "Take this signboard bearing the words 'Dead to public opinion' and wear it a few hours in the center of town." Is that how we become dead to the world? Although one would not deny the probable benefits of that experience, it is not an adequate answer to the question.

The key to being dead to the world is the same as the key to being dead to sin and dead to self. What led to the

DEAD TO THE WORLD

severance of Paul's relationship to the world? Remember his testimony in Galatians 6:14. Paul's identifying with Jesus and His cross-inflicted death brought about a changed attitude toward the world. Colossians 2:20 contains the same answer in these terms: "If ye be dead with Christ from [or *to*] the rudiments of the world . . . "

God's way for our becoming dead to the world is by becoming a cross-bearing disciple of Christ. Since we cannot serve two masters, our coming under the lordship of Jesus Christ will spell death to our love for the world. Attachment to Christ is the secret of detachment from the world. If you are having a problem with loving the world, there is something wrong with your attachment to Christ. It is just that simple.

Jesus spoke of the necessity of every disciple taking up *his own* cross. That cross you take up is the cross on which you will die to the world. My meeting the terms of discipleship as I follow Christ in daily life puts me out of step with nondisciples. It brings me into head-on collision with those who do not submit to the Lord Jesus Christ. There is a parting of ways. It is inevitable, for we cannot serve two masters. Often a breach is created between us and those of our friends and relatives who are Christian in name only. This suffering that

Dying to Live With Christ

one experiences as a consequence of following Christ constitutes his cross. Any believer can avoid the cross by simply conforming to the world, but that is the sad undoing of his discipleship.

Let us consider some marks of a life that is dead to the world. Some of these will be stated negatively and some positively.

First, one who is dead to the world is oblivious to both the world's praise and the world's ridicule. He is neither inflated by its praise, nor hurt by its ridicule.

Here is the testimony of George Mueller: "There was a day when I died—died to George Mueller, his opinions, preferences, his tastes, and will; died to the world, its approval or censure; . . . and since then I have studied only to show myself approved unto God."

Second, he who is dead to the world will never sacrifice kingdom interests on the altar of worldly success. Unlike Balaam, he will be bribed by neither wealth nor position.

When President Coolidge asked the missionary John Mott to serve as this country's ambassador to Japan, the reply he received was this: "Mr. President, since God called me to be an ambassador of His, my ears have been deaf to all other calls." He was single-minded. He

DEAD TO THE WORLD

was determined to serve only the Lord. He could not be bribed into sacrificing kingdom interests on any altar. May that challenge us to a similar singleness of heart.

Third, one who is dead to the world makes very little ado about his earthly citizenship. Here is a paragraph that explains this verity.

"These disciples keep themselves free from the politics of this world. They do not consider themselves as called to battle against any form of government or ideology. They can operate under any form of government and be loyal to that government up to the point where they are required to compromise their testimony or deny their Lord. Then they refuse to obey, and submit to the consequences rather than stir up a revolution."

Fourth, the fads and fashions of the world will exert absolutely no influence upon one who is dead to the world. Jesus Christ, the one whom we follow, has given us very clear directions: "Be not conformed to this world." "It is your duty," wrote Charles Finney, "to dress so plain as to show to the world that you place no sort of reliance in the things of fashion, and set no value at all on them, but despise and neglect them altogether."

Many professing Christians are so alive to the world that they would rather be indecent than different. But

Dying to Live With Christ

the supposedly conservative sister who constantly experiments with new dresses and new dress patterns, copying the renovations of others, is likewise manifesting a worldly spirit.

Fifth, one who is dead to the world will demonstrate by frugality and simplicity his deliverance from the tyranny of things. Being a stranger and pilgrim in this world, he will live simply. His eye will be blind to the niceties and luxuries that captivate so many. He will learn to make do with less than the best. One of the deceptions of our day is that happiness lies in the accumulation of things. But the person who is dead to the world will not seek to find happiness there.

Sixth, one who is dead to the world will not pile up excess baggage as though he had here a continuing city. Ignoring the counsel of the world and taking seriously the call to forsake all, he will keep his material and economic assets to a functional minimum. A pervading sense of stewardship will make him a generous giver. He will adopt the economic philosophy of William Carey: "My business is being a Christian. I cobble shoes to pay expenses." We need more of that philosophy in our circles.

Seventh, when one is dead to the world, its pleasures find him unresponsive. Two newly converted girls received

DEAD TO THE WORLD

from their former companions an invitation to attend a dance. Their reply, as nearly as I can recollect, was, "We can't come; we're dead; we got converted last week."

Let us look next at some symptoms that indicate too much aliveness to the world.

In the first place, beware of an unwarranted fear of becoming radical. True Christianity is, in a real sense, radical in the eyes of many. Some people seem more afraid of what they call extremes than of sin! They are so afraid of getting out on a limb that they never get up the tree, spiritually.

Second, beware of a cheap consecration that lacks the dimension of sacrifice. Cheap service gives the Lord less than our best. Less than our all is a worldly attitude. Jesus set forth a principle of the kingdom when He said, "Except a corn of wheat fall into the ground and die, it abideth alone: but if it die, it bringeth forth much fruit." When we cease to bleed, we cease to bless. There is a lot of "service" rendered today, but much of it is worldly service, in contrast to Christian service.

Third, beware when you become too easily distracted. Deadness to the world will be reflected in a preoccupation with the cause of Christ. Until He comes, we are to "occupy" in a spirit of undistracted loyalty.

Dying to Live With Christ

Peter's question, "What shall this man do?" earned for him a rebuke from the Lord. He was too alive to things that should not have distracted him.

Fourth, beware of allowing human relations and sentimental ties to come between you and the Lord. "He that loveth father or mother . . . and . . . son or daughter more than me is not worthy of me." Some well-meaning parents have made statements like this: "You'll break your mother's heart if you leave me to go to the mission field." That is nearer to a worldly spirit than we may realize.

Fifth, if you are strongly opinionated, hungry for power, contentious, or divisive, beware. That is the spirit of the world, the way of the Gentiles. They love to exercise lordship, but the Christian way to unity is through humility.

Last, beware if you have not been delivered from carnal fear—the fear of man. "The fear of man bringeth a snare" (Proverbs 29:25). Being afraid to do what we know we should do is carnal fear. It is worldly to cave in to peer pressure. We need to be more like the man of whom it was said, "He feared man so little, because he feared God so much."

Upon their arrival on a certain island, a group of

DEAD TO THE WORLD

missionaries was warned, "These natives might kill you." They replied, "We died before we came." That is the kind of human material that God can use to His honor and glory.

Are we dead to worldly fears, or are we afraid to be different? Are we so afraid of spoiling our relationship with some individuals that we hesitate to witness to them of the goodness of the Lord?

This has been a look at some of the less obvious symptoms of worldliness. God's plan includes not only getting us out of the world but also getting the world out of us. God help us to be willing to say, "Take the world, but give me Jesus."

That like as Christ was raised up from the dead by the glory of the Father, even so we also should walk in newness of life.
Romans 6:4

4.

RISEN WITH CHRIST

Most people in the depths of their hearts, know and have known, how they ought to live and what they ought to do. Their problem is that either they do not want to do it, or they do not have the power to do what they know they ought to do.

Paul, the apostle, spoke for the latter group when in anguish of soul he poured out his inner feelings in words of near despair. "O wretched man that I am! who shall deliver me?" Another has voiced his need in these words: "I need a man to rise within me that the man I am might cease to be." This human problem has engaged many

Dying to Live With Christ

of the keenest minds of all time, but all the proposed humanistic solutions have proven futile. The best that science can do is to add years to man's life. It cannot add life to man's years.

This is precisely what God through Christ stands ready to do: "I am come," Jesus said, "that they might have life, and that they might have it more abundantly" (John 10:10). But in so many instances, man comes to an acceptance of God's way only after a long series of disappointing attempts. Romans 7 is a reflection of this long and bitter struggle. As we come to know God, we learn that He is in the business of shattering the idols that men worship so that they might turn back to Him.

Many are the idols that men worship, but the idol of self is possibly the one that men cling to most tenaciously. Since God's way demands death to self, there is a natural shrinking back from that way. For man's encouragement, God, in His Word, holds up repeatedly the hope-inspiring truth that there is a new and risen life just beyond the death that self so much shrinks from. George Matheson put that truth in these words:

> "O cross that liftest up my head,
> I dare not ask to hide from thee;

RISEN WITH CHRIST

>I lay in dust life's glory dead,
>And from the ground there blossoms red,
>Life that shall endless be."

God, through the redeeming work of His Son, made provision for the uniting of every repentant sinner with the Saviour. On the manward side, that potential becomes real in one's experience when in faith and repentance he surrenders himself to the Lord Jesus. From that point onward, assuming he remains faithful, that person is viewed by God as being one with Christ.

One of the greatest assertions of this truth occurs in Ephesians 2:4–6: "But God, who is rich in mercy, for His great love wherewith He loved us, even when we were dead in sins, hath quickened us together with Christ . . . and hath raised us up together, and made us sit together in heavenly places." *Together,* in this instance, means "you together with Christ!"

This is a precious truth. On the Godward side, a spiritual union is formed between the believer and Christ that is beyond the power of the senses to perceive, and yet it is very real. We are told elsewhere that "the things which are seen are temporal; but the things which are not seen are eternal" (2 Corinthians 4:18). Temporal things are less enduring and less important than the

Dying to Live With Christ

things that the senses cannot perceive. The union of the believer with the Lord Jesus is a fact that we could never have discovered. It is known only because God revealed it.

As the newborn saint identifies closely with Christ in a life of discipleship, his life pattern is changed radically. The old life of sin is laid off. A new life of holiness is put on. By means of this sanctifying process, the potential oneness of the saint with his Saviour becomes a reality on the experiential level. Romans 6:4 has this purpose of God in view. "Like as Christ was raised up from the dead by the glory of the Father, even so we also should walk in newness of life."

The overall purpose of Romans 6 is to show how life does indeed become different as oneness with Christ becomes a reality. The pattern of change follows the actual experience of Christ. As Christ died *for* sin, the responding one dies *to* sin. As Christ was resurrected from the tomb, the responding one is resurrected from his sinful state. As Christ ascended into the heights of heaven, the responding one is lifted into the heights of holiness. It can therefore be said that Christianity is a repetition of the resurrection of Christ that occurs in the realm of the human spirit.

RISEN WITH CHRIST

There are three words in Romans 6 that highlight the responsibility of the responding believer. Those three key words are *know, reckon,* and *yield.* Our knowing, reckoning, and yielding will bring about a dying to self, sin, and the world.

Thus far, we have been emphasizing the negative aspect of sanctification, and that aspect of Christian experience is indispensable. However, it must be admitted that dead men are negative. Being dead, they do not respond to temptation or pride, and that is commendable; but that is not enough. Dead men do not fill the world with song and cheer and love. Dead men do not become missionaries and agents of God's grace, and it is not God's plan that we be simply dead to sin. There is a positive experience with Christ that follows death to the old man. That is the focus of this chapter.

Among the familiar words heard at a graveside are these: "Blessed are the dead which die in the Lord." Will you allow me for a moment to take that out of its context? "Blessed are the dead which die in the Lord" is gloriously true in another sense. Blessings unmeasurable do indeed rest upon those who in the Lord die to self, sin, and the world. Resurrections follow immediately in the wake of that kind of dying.

Dying to Live With Christ

Many towns have a shop in them where clothing can be dyed a different color. In front of one such shop, there once hung a sign bearing these words: "I dye to live. I live to dye. The more I dye, the more I live. The more I live, the more I dye." This use of *dye* in place of *die* was proper. But as the sign was verbalized, it carried a double meaning. Whether aware of it or not, that shop owner was publicizing also the spiritual truth that lies embedded in Romans 6.

When one begins to reckon himself dead to sin and alive unto God, he will have his own Gethsemane, his own Golgotha. But praise God, he will also have his own resurrection to newness of life! The promise is that if we have been planted together in the likeness of His death, we shall be also in the likeness of His resurrection.

Earlier, we indicated that by virtue of the believer's union with Christ, he is born crucified. Now we are emphasizing the positive counterpart of that negative. By virtue of that same union, the believer is born resurrected! Although we do need to identify with Christ in death, our union is with a living, risen Christ.

An interesting sequence occurs in Romans 5, 6, and 8. In chapter 5 the key preposition is that little word *for*. "Christ died *for* the ungodly." In chapter 6 the emphasis

RISEN WITH CHRIST

moves to another preposition, *with*. "Our old man is crucified *with* him." Then in chapter 8, the key word is still another preposition, *in*. "There is therefore now no condemnation to them which are *in* Christ Jesus." We can experience the risen life because of our being in union with the risen Christ.

Let us pursue now, in Romans 6, the outworking of the risen life, beginning with verse 11: "Likewise reckon ye also yourselves to be dead indeed unto sin, but alive unto God through Jesus Christ our Lord. Let not sin therefore reign in your mortal body, that ye should obey it in the lusts thereof. Neither yield ye your members as instruments of unrighteousness unto sin: but yield yourselves unto God, as those that are alive from the dead, and your members as instruments of righteousness unto God. For sin shall not have dominion over you: for ye are not under the law, but under grace. What then? shall we sin, because we are not under the law, but under grace? God forbid. Know ye not, that to whom ye yield yourselves servants to obey, his servants ye are to whom ye obey; whether of sin unto death, or of obedience unto righteousness? But God be thanked, that ye were the servants of sin, but ye have obeyed from the heart that form of doctrine which was delivered you.

Dying to Live With Christ

Being then made free from sin, ye became the servants of righteousness." The emphasis here is on the third of these three key ideas. Knowing and reckoning should lead to yielding.

Let us compare the three ideas. *Knowing* relates to faith. God intends that we believe His declarations. They give us the Gospel facts that we need to know. But the commands of God call for a different response, an action response rather than a faith response. In Romans 6 the words *reckon* and *yield* appear in commands that are addressed to the will. They call for obedience, and verse 17 speaks of obeying from the heart. This obedient yielding is proof that one is reckoning on what God has said and done.

In simple terms, the risen life becomes a reality as one ignores his former masters and obeys his new Master. Sin's reign over us is broken as we yield to the all-victorious, indwelling Christ. This yielding can be and should be a joyful yielding, like the yielding of a bride to her lover. This, in fact, is the very figure employed in the next chapter, Romans 7. Verse 4 declares that the newborn Christian is "married to another, even to him who is raised from the dead." This speaks of a close union.

Although we do not claim to have arrived at a state of

RISEN WITH CHRIST

sinless perfection, we are no longer slaves to sin. If we stumble and fall, we get up again and go on. Our former master called us to lie down in sin and enjoy it. Our new master awakens us to the fact that the wages of sin is death. He imparts to us newness of life and resistance to sin. The risen life is a life of victory over all the enemies of holiness, but it is not a once-for-all victory. It is rather a moment-by-moment, day-by-day victory.

It is significant that the terms *reckon* and *yield* are in the present imperative form. The best rendering would therefore be "Keep on reckoning; keep on yielding." Without this cooperation, even Christ cannot save a sinner and make of him a saint.

Paul was both a salvationist and a disciplinarian. He made much of salvation by grace through faith, but he also spoke unapologetically of the urgency of crucifying the flesh and mortifying the deeds of the body. It is the practice of this Holy Spirit-energized discipline that keeps the old man and his deeds inoperative, and provides the soil out of which the new life can blossom forth in beauty and power.

Remember the principle "The more I die, the more I live." Someone has made this significant observation: "The climax of the risen life gravitates, strange to say,

Dying to Live With Christ

back to the cross." As was previously stated, one never graduates from the dead-with-Christ state. There must be the reckoning of ourselves dead to sin along with the reckoning of ourselves alive unto God. Paul, the apostle, in one of his personal testimonies, said, "I have suffered the loss of all things, . . . that I may know him, and the power of his resurrection, and the fellowship of his sufferings, being made conformable unto his death." One of the strongest proofs that the power of the resurrection is operating in your life lies in a willingness to voluntarily share the fellowship of Christ's sufferings and be made conformable unto His death.

The latter part of Romans 6 teaches repeatedly that whether one is a saint or a sinner, he is by creation a servant. Even becoming a saint does not change the fact that we are servants by creation. The difference, however, between the saint and the sinner lies in their having a different master.

Those who continue to yield to the devil soon lose the freedom they once had. Life for them becomes a series of ruts from which they cannot escape. On the contrary, those who choose to yield their allegiance to the Lord Jesus retain their original endowment of freedom and gain even more because where the Spirit of the Lord is,

RISEN WITH CHRIST

there is liberty"—the glorious liberty of the children of God.

True freedom is not doing as you please, but doing as you ought. There are a lot of people who do not have the power to do that. Only the person who is vitally linked to the triumphant Christ has a sufficient inner dynamic to live as he knows he ought, and that is true freedom.

An attempt will now be made to enumerate some further marks of the risen life.

First, it should be emphasized that the risen life is a divinely conferred life. A new life is planted in the believer—one that operates under the control of divine principles. According to 1 Corinthians 15:45, Christ "was made a quickening spirit." He not only possesses eternal life Himself, but He also imparts that life to others.

When speaking to Martha, Jesus said, "I am the resurrection, and the life: he that believeth in me . . . shall never die." He lives to give life, and the life He gives is of a quality that survives the experience of physical death.

So then the spiritual life of the regenerate person is extraneous. Its seat is not in himself; he is not spiritually self-subsistent. He lives by virtue of his union with Christ. This is a fact often overlooked in

Dying to Live With Christ

Calvinistic circles. "This is the record," John says, "that God hath given to us eternal life, and this life is in his Son. He that hath the Son hath life; and he that hath not the Son of God hath not life" (1 John 5:11, 12). Ever since the day of Pentecost when the Spirit of Christ was poured out on His followers, a new quality of life has been experienced by believing men and women. It is the life of the resurrected Saviour, communicated by His Spirit, who indwells the believer.

There is a legend which says that wherever Jesus walked, flowers sprang up in His footprints. While that is mere legend, the spiritual equivalent of that does occur. In many a spot the desert of life begins to blossom as a rose. Dead sticks, like Aaron's rod, begin to bud. Lives that were once shriveled and drab begin to sprout with life, vitality, and hope.

Second, the risen life is markedly different from one's former life. The change begins on the inside and is intended to continue until all of life has been touched. "If any man be in Christ, he is a new creature," a new creation. He has a new life, a new Master, and therefore a new purpose in life. He now sets his affections on things above; therefore, he has new interests.

When the members of Christ described the difference

RISEN WITH CHRIST

that Christ had made in their lives, they put it like this: "We have passed from death unto life." As the non-Christian observes us, does he see that great a change? He may not be able to see how different we are on the inside, but he ought to be able to tell from what he sees on the outside that we must be different on the inside.

Third, the risen life is a life of beauty, fullness, and power. As the Spirit of God begins to permeate the life of the newborn believer, the attractive fruit of the Spirit becomes manifest: love, joy, peace, long-suffering, and so on. As one of the branches in the vine, the believer becomes a channel through which Christ pours out His life unto others. Through union with Christ, life becomes beautiful and fruitful.

There is an allegory about a gardener who dug an old briar out of a ditch, transplanted it into his garden, and then using a sharp knife, budded it with a rose. Before long, lovely roses were blooming where once there had been only briars. The gardener then supposedly said, "Your beauty is due, not to what came out of you, but to what I put into you."

Thus it is with the Christian. We resembled that ugly briar. But Jesus, the rose of Sharon, has come into our lives, and all the difference is due to His presence. Was

Dying to Live With Christ

it not prophesied, "Instead of the brier shall come up the myrtle tree"? There is beauty in place of ugliness, all because of our oneness with Christ.

The same power becomes operative in our lives as was operative in the resurrection of Jesus from the dead. That is why Paul prayed as he did for the Ephesians, that they might know "the exceeding greatness of his power to us-ward who believe, according to the working of his mighty power, which he wrought in Christ, when he raised him from the dead." There is available resurrection power for the risen life!

Fourth, the risen life is a life of companionship with the living Christ. After Jesus told His disciples of His coming death, He added, "I will not leave you comfortless: I will come to you." That promise was fulfilled on the day of Pentecost when Jesus returned to be, not merely *with* them as before, but now *in* them in the person of the Holy Spirit. A Christian who was asked to explain to a non-Christian why his life was different, replied in these words, "You live your life alone; I don't." That awareness of divine companionship should be the possession of every child of God. A peddler once called at a Christian's home. The lady received him into her home and began to testify immediately by

RISEN WITH CHRIST

saying, "It is wonderful to be saved." The peddler, to her surprise, replied, "Yes, but I know something better." The astonished lady wondered what that could be, to which the visitor replied, "To have the companionship of the risen Christ is better than knowing that one is saved." The human problem of loneliness finds its answer in the risen life.

Finally, the risen life is a life of conquest. That is how it is depicted in Romans 5, verse 17: "For if by one man's offence death reigned by one; much more they which receive abundance of grace and of the gift of righteousness shall reign in life by one, Jesus Christ." Our reigning in life is a direct outcome of Christ reigning in us, and that is when life reaches its highest pinnacle. May God teach us how to live on the resurrection side of the cross. Then the world at its worst will see the church at its best.